I TRAVEL GUIDE 2023

The Ultimate Pocket Guide to the Eternal City: Discover the Ancient history, Art, Food and Culture of Romans. Everything you Need to Know Before Plan a Trip to Rome.

STUART HARTLEY

© Copyright 2023. All Rights Reserved.

The publication is sold with the idea that the publisher is not required to render accounting, officially permitted or otherwise qualified services. This document is geared towards providing exact and reliable information concerning the topic and issue covered. If advice is necessary, legal or professional, a practiced individual in the profession should be ordered.

- From a Declaration of Principles which was accepted and approved equally by a Committee of the American Bar Association and a Committee of Publishers and Associations.

In no way is it legal to reproduce, duplicate, or transmit any part of this document in either electronic means or printed format. Recording of this publication is strictly prohibited, and any storage of this document is not allowed unless with written permission from the publisher—all rights reserved.

The information provided herein is stated to be truthful and consistent. Any liability, in terms of inattention or otherwise, by any usage or abuse of any policies, processes, or directions contained within is the sole and utter responsibility of the recipient reader. Under no circumstances will any legal responsibility or blame be held against the publisher for any reparation, damages, or monetary loss due to the information herein, either directly or indirectly.

Respective authors own all copyrights not held by the publisher.

The information herein is offered for informational purposes solely and is universal as so. The presentation of the information is without a contract or any guarantee assurance.

The trademarks that are used are without any consent, and the publication of the trademark is without permission or backing by the trademark owner. All trademarks and brands within this book are for clarifying purposes only and are owned by the owners themselves, not affiliated with this document

TABLE OF CONTENTS

INTRODUCTION	5
CHAPTERS 1: HISTORIC PLACES	11
THE COLOSSEUM	15
THE SISTINE CHAPEL	20
TREVI FOUNTAIN	23
PIAZZA NAVONA	26
PANTHEON	28
ROMAN FORUM	31
THE SPANISH STEPS	35
CIRCUS MAXIMUS.	37
OSTIA ANTICA	39
THE CATACOMBS	41
CHAPTERS 2: MUSEUMS AND ART GALLERIES	44
NATIONAL ROMAN MUSEUM	47
THE BORGHESE GALLERY	48
THE NATIONAL GALLERY OF ANCIENT ART.	50
CHAPTERS 3: CUISINE AND WINE	52
TYPICAL DISHES	53
LOCAL WINES	59
RECOMMENDED RESTAURANTS	69
CHAPTERS 4: ACTIVITIES AND ENTERTAINMENT	70
SHOPPING	73
MARKETS	74
WALKS ALONG THE TIBER, AND PARKS AND GARDENS	76
CHAPTER 5: WALKING ITINERARIES	77

LOCATIONS TO VISIT	80
TOURIST SPOTS AND ATTRACTIONS,	83
CHAPTER 6: LODGING AND TRANSPORTATION	85
TYPES OF LODGING AVAILABLE IN ROME	89
INFORMATION ON TRANSPORTATION AVAILABLE FOR GETTING AROUND.	91
CONCLUSION	93

INTRODUCTION

Europe is an amazing wonderland of hypnotic beauty, carefree, friendly life, and rich historical significance. Its rustic plains of Spain, snow-laden slopes of Switzerland, and modern masterpieces like the Eiffel tower in Paris. One will never want to want to go back home from there. This continent is home to various cultures, delicious foods, and fascinating people.

Great sights and activities may be found in that old city. Here, the art comes in a variety of powerful, interesting styles. Rome is also the most significant city in western antiquity and the birthplace of European civilization, where the past and present coexist. Travelers fall in love with Rome because of its distinctive characteristics, including the spectacular thrill of its many years of stormy history, natural occurrences, and architectural gems created by the greatest historical artists.

Rome is a particularly impressive city, largely because of its historic buildings. Rome, the Eternal City, is one of the world's most historically rich and culturally diverse cities. Rome has been a major center of civilization for over two and a half thousand years because of its stunning architecture, vibrant culture, and rich history.

Rome is one of the biggest cities in Italy and the capital of Lazio. Rome is one of the oldest towns in Italy, with a history that dates back almost three thousand years. Today, Rome is one of the most popular tourist destinations in the world. It currently ranks third in EU visits, behind London and Paris, and welcomes about 10 million visitors annually. Rome is one of the principal locations for archaeological study and research worldwide.

From the Colosseum, one of the world's most iconic ruins, to the magnificent Vatican Museums, the city is home to an unparalleled collection of art, sculpture, and architecture. Visitors can stroll through the winding streets of the historic center, taste the famous Italian cuisine, and explore the many famous landmarks, including the Roman Forum, Trevi Fountain, and the Spanish Steps. With its timeless beauty, rich history, and vibrant energy, Rome is truly a city like no other.

Italy's pulsating center is Rome. A modern capital in every way while also being steeped in history, it has many art, architecture, and religion to appeal to every tourist, traveler, scholar, or pilgrim.

Rome has a rich and storied history that spans thousands of years. It was founded in 753 BCE and became the capital of the Roman Republic in the 4th century BCE. Rome was the center of a vast empire that stretched across Europe, Africa, and the Near East during its heyday. Today, the city is home to many of the most famous ruins and monuments from this period, including the Colosseum, the Roman Forum, and the Pantheon.

While various individuals visit Rome differently, there are several sights that one should never miss. The Coliseum is the city's most well-known landmark, and you must go there. You can either explore it on your own or hire a guide included in the organized excursions. The tour guides don gladiator garb. You should phone ahead and ask about these trips because their start time is not set.

Rome is a captivating location that draws visitors because of its extensive cultural history and magnificent ancient landmarks.

Rome has always been a popular destination for its historic structures and rich culture. The city, located on the western leg of Italy, has been inhabited for 2,700 years.

Rome is the ideal study travel location for students learning about ancient history and classical civilizations because it was one of the mightiest centers of power in the ancient world and is a fascinating palimpsest of history, religion, and culture spanning the periods. Some of the most impressive monuments from the ancient world may still be seen amid this constantly intriguing, multilayered city's present bustle, and there is still much to be learned from them.

Rome is a city that celebrates its rich cultural heritage, from its art and architecture to its food and fashion. It is renowned for its museums and galleries, including the Vatican Museums, which house some of the world's most famous works of art. The city is famous for its street performers, outdoor markets, and vibrant nightlife.

Because the city has American and European traditions, Rome in Italy is renowned for having two sides of the coin as its facade. Rome is considered as one of the world's best and most well-known ancient cities and one of the most distinctive in all of Europe among its neighbors. Rome has so much to offer tourists that it is impossible to see and explore it all in one day.

Rome is full of ancient traditions that are still celebrated today. For example, the Feast of the Epiphany (La Befana) is an important event in the city's calendar, as is Carnevale, a pre-Lenten festival famous for its colorful parades and elaborate costumes. Easter week is also a significant time, with traditional processions and ceremonies occurring throughout the city. In addition, Rome is renowned for its cuisine, with traditional dishes such as pasta carbonara and saltimbocca alla Romana, reflecting the city's long culinary heritage.

Rome is a wonderful city! Rome is undoubtedly the ideal location for any traveler because it is a city where the past and the present coexist in style. Rome is the ideal setting, whether your goal is to visit all major sites in order or want to kick back and relax.

Travelers seeking art, history, culture, romance, and entertainment should head to Rome. Rome shines at you from every direction, day and night, with a luminous contentment that is pure self-wonder at the astounding depth of knowledge and wisdom it offers. It is a 24-hour city, with theaters, restaurants, and pubs just waiting to be discovered at night, in addition to museums, galleries, and monuments that can be seen during the day.

Rome is home to many well-known landmarks, but the city also contains some hidden gems. Rome was not built in a day, nor can its tourist attractions. Take your time; it will wait while you treat it right because it has been there for almost three millennia.

Rome (established in 753 BC) is today proud of its vast historical and cultural history. Rome was born on seven hills (Capitoline, Quirinal (Quirinale), Esquilino, Viminale, Celia, Palatine, and Aventine), crisscrossed by the River Tiber.

Right now, Roma is divided into two main sections: the inner, or historical core, encircled by the Aurelian walls, which were constructed at the end of the third century AD to fence off the Seven Hills, and the neighborhood or suburban region.

The State of Vatican City, the seat of the Catholic Church's papacy, is located inside the boundaries of the Comune of Rome. The Lateran Pacts, signed by the Italian government in 1929, recognized Vatican City as an independent state. Its area is 42 m2, and there are about 1,000 individuals that live there. On the city's horizon is the magnificent St. Peter's Basilica, which houses the largest dome in the world.

Rome is most enjoyable to visit in April, May, October, and November. The fields surrounding the city have a magnificent landscape at these times, and the weather is comfortable. Tourists should aim to avoid August because it is the month when most Italians take vacations, and as a result, many stores are closed. Even while it can get very chilly during the winter, the sun shines regularly, fewer people are around, and prices are significantly lower.

Rome, the capital of modern Italy, is home to several excellent cafes and restaurants, fantastic nightlife, and vibrant squares and streets. Despite being a large city, the historic district is not too large. This Rome travel guide offers thorough guidance and travel information.

Let's get started!

CHAPTERS 1: HISTORIC PLACES

Rome is home to many well-known landmarks, but the city also contains some hidden gems. Rome was not built in a day, nor can its tourist attractions. Take your time; it will wait while you treat it right because it has been there for almost three millennia.

Rome is known as the Città Eterna, or eternal city, since its history spans nearly the entirety of human history, at least 800 years before the birth of Christ. With a population of more than one million, the Roman Empire was the biggest in the world at its peak. Rome is exceptional in that it is divided among two independent sovereign states.

The Pope, the nominal leader of the Roman Catholic Church across the globe, is housed at the Holy See, which administers the area of Vatican City. The Sovereign Military Order of Malta (SMOM), whose citizens fled to Rome in 1834, is the second state. The SMOM's legality in Rome is in question because it no longer possesses any territory, and Napoleon Bonaparte's invasion forces forced it to cede its territory in Malta. Rome is such an old city that many of its attractions are ancient, but they coexist alongside the modern. Few visitors will pay attention to that claim, though.

No matter your history, Rome has something to offer you.

Rome is a lovely destination and one of the most romantic cities in the world. One should visit several attractions in Rome, including some of the most well-known architectural marvels, fountains, museums, and art galleries.

A few historic monuments, Renaissance and medieval buildings, fountains, and sizable museums may all be found in Rome. Rome, the capital of modern Italy, is home to several excellent cafes and restaurants, fantastic nightlife, and vibrant squares and streets.

This fashionable metropolis bears the imprint of more than 2,000 years of history everywhere you look. According to legend, Romulus established the City on Palatino, one of the seven hills on which Rome is situated next to the Tevere river. As a result, no matter where you are in the city, you will always have a breathtaking view of it.

A comfortable pair of shoes is the most important item in Rome! It is not necessary to take a bus to visit all the sites in this city.

The entire area resembles a vast, colorful open-air museum. Italians are nice people, so if you are on a street corner with a map in your hand and a bewildered expression, expert assistance. When in Rome, fashion is the name of the game. Wear solid, but not flashy, colors; a scarf flipped stylishly over, and a smart bag over your shoulder. Avoid fanny packs at all costs; they ruin the look of your Gucci!

Avoid eating at tourist cafés near popular locations like St. Mark's Square because they are frequently pricey and offer subpar food and service. You can find better, more affordable cuisine and a chance to eat and converse with the Romans by going back a few streets to the small cafés that the locals frequent.

COLOSSEUM: This enormous open-air stadium could accommodate up to 50,000 Romans and is arguably Rome's most well-known landmark. Built by Emperor Titus in AD80, it served as a venue for gladiatorial fights and games. It even could be submerged underwater to serve as a backdrop for recreations of famous naval wars.

SISTINE CHAPEL: The chapel, which is located far from the Vatican Museums and is a day trip in and of itself, needed some adornment, so in 1508 Michelangelo was hired to paint the 10,000 square-foot ceiling by himself. The finished product, which took more than four years to create, is regarded as one of the world's greatest works of art.

Fontana di Trevi, often known as the Trevi Fountain, is a huge and magnificent fountain from the eighteenth century that Nicola Salvi constructed. If you toss a coin into the fountain with your right hand over your left shoulder, you will someday return to Rome.

PIAZZA NAVONA: This square got its peculiar shape from the original horsemanship arena established there. It is today a bustling, exciting area full of stalls and cafés during the day and portrait and caricature artists during the evening.

The Pantheon was a massive temple that Hadrian completed around 120 AD. Up until 1960, its dome was the largest in the world. The original doors are now approximately 1,900 years old and are still present. A stunning and fascinating structure.

THE VATICAN'S PAPAL BASILICA OF SAINT PETER: The Papal Basilica of Saint Peter in the Vatican, also called Saint Peter's Basilica or the Basilica Papale di San Pietro in Vaticano is a Late Renaissance basilica situated within Vatican City. Donato Bramante, Michelangelo, Carlo Maderno, and Gian Lorenzo Bernini were mostly responsible for the design. According to Roman Catholic belief, Saint Peter, one of Jesus' twelve apostles, is buried in the basilica that bears his name.

Travestere is a unique neighborhood with meandering lanes and little shops offering interesting and strange items, wonderful nightlife food, and a sizable Sunday market. It is not the main tourist area of Rome, and the alleged oldest Church in Rome is also located there. The stunning Santa Maria's oldest section is thought to have been built in the third century AD.

The largest parkland area in Rome, Villa Borghese, is a great spot to escape the bustle of the city for a bit. There are wonderful art galleries, peaceful walks, a lake where you may rent a boat, and lovely trees. Every July, it also presents classical music performances outside.

Numerous walking tours are available, and they're a terrific opportunity to see the city's highlights while being accompanied by an enthusiastic and informed guide.

Be wary of overzealous street vendors in well-known tourist attractions like the Trevi fountain.

Even though the city is generally safe, staying on the main streets at night is recommended. These are usual sights in and of themselves as the fashionable locals head out for a promenade and a satisfying lunch. A fantastic time to people-watch, especially if you're sitting at one of the outdoor tables many cafes and restaurants have.

However, the major attraction of any trip to Rome should always be the city's unique architecture and history.

THE COLOSSEUM

Rome is one of the most stunning cities in the world to visit, with amazing architecture, well-known artwork, and intriguing history.

One of Rome's most well-known structures is the Coliseum, where thousands of gladiator matches and other martial spectacles took place to entertain the Roman populace. The Coliseum is an extremely well-liked attraction; thus, the lines can be long. You may sign up for several guided tours to skip the lines and learn a little bit about the history of the Coliseum. It would help if you searched for some of these trips online to ensure a spot.

The enormous amphitheater in the heart of Rome is fittingly called the Colosseum. More than 50,000 people saw the gladiators battle to death in ancient Rome. It was the biggest amphitheater the Romans had ever constructed and was in operation for more than 600 years. A monument of scale would have dominated the ancient Rome skyline. These days, various modern theatre productions are presented here, along with recreations of famous wars. Even then, the Romans understood the influence of propaganda. They knew their power was artificial, even though they had been considered unbeatable for almost a thousand years.

Due to extensive earthquake damage, the Colosseum is mostly destroyed, although there is still enough of it to remind us of its historical significance. Since it ceased as an amphitheater, it has served as a quarry, a church, a castle, and other things. The Roman Catholic Cardinal Altieri authorized its usage to host bullfights in the seventeenth century, but the idea was abandoned due to public outcry. It was dedicated and is now home to the Stations of the Cross after the Church adopted it as a memorial for early Christian martyrs.

The 21st century has seen protests against the death penalty. Given its imperial past, the nighttime illumination is now changed from white to gold if a death sentence is commuted anywhere in the world.

Colosseum first is a massive structure that dates back to when Rome was the center of the world and enslaved people fought for their freedom within its wide, convex walls.

The Colosseum, also known as the Flavian Amphitheatre, is an iconic landmark in Rome, Italy. It was built during the reign of the Flavian emperors as a venue for gladiatorial contests and public spectacles. With a seating capacity of over 50,000 people, the Colosseum was the largest amphitheater in the ancient world.

Construction of the Colosseum began in 70-80 AD and was completed in 80 AD. The building was made of concrete and stone, characterized by its elliptical shape, tiered seating, and the network of tunnels and rooms used to support the various spectacles.

Colosseum has undergone significant damage and changes over the centuries, but much of its original structure remains today. The Colosseum is now a major tourist attraction and a symbol of Rome and the Roman Empire. Visitors can tour the inside of the Colosseum, which provides an immersive experience of the history and architecture of one of the world's most iconic buildings.

The Colosseum is an iconic landmark in Rome, Italy, and it was built as an amphitheater for gladiatorial contests and public spectacles. Here's a quick guide for visiting the Colosseum:

LOCATION: The Colosseum is located in the center of Rome, in the archaeological area known as the Roman Forum.

OPENING HOURS: It is open daily from 8:30 am to 4:30 pm, with extended hours during the summer.

TICKET INFORMATION: You can purchase tickets in advance on the official Colosseum website or at the ticket office on the day of your visit. Admission also includes access to the Roman Forum and Palatine Hill.

TOUR OPTIONS: Guided tours of the Colosseum are available, which provide a deeper insight into the history and architecture of the building.

ACCESSIBILITY: The Colosseum is accessible for visitors with mobility limitations, with ramps and elevators available.

SAFETY MEASURES: Due to COVID-19, safety measures such as face masks and social distancing are mandatory inside the Colosseum.

WHAT TO SEE: The Colosseum is famous for its architectural design and rich history, with many notable features to explore, including the arena floor, the hypogeum (underground level), and the various tiers of seating.

For stunning pictures of this beautiful monument and Constantine's Arch lit up, try scheduling a visit at night as well. A tour is advised if you want to learn more about the area than take beautiful pictures; they are not always overpriced and can provide interesting background information.

Visiting the Colosseum is a unique experience that provides a glimpse into the history and culture of ancient Rome. Enjoy your visit!

THE SISTINE CHAPEL

Visit the Sistine Chapel in the Vatican for a culturally rich and highly revered location if you want to discover more about Rome. The Vatican museums are also a must-see because they contain all of the history and the magnificent Gallery of Tapestries, leaving you in awe of the meticulous attention to detail that went into these magnificent works. If you're unfamiliar with the history, the Vatican offers a Sistine Chapel and Vatican museum tour, which I highly suggest. The cost of the guided tours is about 30 euros.

Some of the most expensive pieces of commissioned art ever are found in the Sistine Chapel. After convincing Michelangelo to paint the chapel's ceiling, Pope Sixtus IV della Rovere gave the building its current name, Cappella Sistina (between 1477 and 1480).

Amazingly, Michelangelo rejected the commission since he considered himself a sculptor. However, the Pope had some persuasive strategies that the rest of us were unaware of, not the least of which was the threat of ex-communication. The Pope ultimately got his way; the rest is history, as they say. Although it is unknown if Michelangelo ever looked back on the project, it did ruin his health. He was in his 60s and would live the rest of his life with neck and back issues.

Although the grandeur of the Sistine Chapel is beyond this article's scope, the paintings on the ceiling were miraculously restored between

1981 and 1993 to remove the centuries' worth of filth in the paint, taking much longer than the initial effort.

For God to evaluate the Pope's soul, his body is deposited in the Sistine Chapel beneath the Last Judgement mural. The chapel is also where the conclave takes place to pick a new pope. Even non-Catholics cannot but be touched by the sheer audacity of the concept as the entire piece tells the tale of humanity and the universe.

The Sistine Chapel is a world-famous site in Vatican City, Rome, Italy. It is renowned for its ceiling, painted by Michelangelo, depicting scenes from the Book of Genesis. Here's a quick travel guide to help you plan your visit:

TIMINGS: The Sistine Chapel is open to visitors daily except Sundays and certain religious holidays. It is usually open from 9:00 am to 6:00 pm, with extended hours in the summer months.

ADMISSION: You can visit the Sistine Chapel as part of a tour of the Vatican Museums or as a standalone visit. Admission to the chapel is included in the Vatican Museums ticket.

DRESS CODE: Visitors must dress modestly when visiting the Sistine Chapel, which means covering your shoulders and knees and avoiding hats and revealing clothing.

GUIDED TOURS: Guided tours are available and can provide you with a more in-depth understanding of the art and history of the Sistine Chapel.

PHOTOGRAPHY: Photography is allowed in the Sistine Chapel, but flash photography is not permitted.

ACCESSIBILITY: The Sistine Chapel is accessible to visitors with disabilities, but some areas may be difficult to access.

In conclusion, visiting the Sistine Chapel is a once-in-a-lifetime experience, and planning can help ensure a smooth and enjoyable visit.

TREVI FOUNTAIN

The Trevi Fountain is a baroque-style fountain located in Rome, Italy. It is one of the world's most famous and beautiful fountains and a symbol of the City of Rome.

The Trevi Fountain was built in the 18th century and is located at the intersection of three roads, where its name, Trevi, comes from (Trevi means "three streets" in Italian). Neptune, the Roman god of the sea, is depicted as a center figure in the fountain, which is surrounded by additional figures and artistic elements.

Visitors to the Trevi Fountain are said to have good luck if they throw a coin into the fountain with their right hand over their left shoulder. According to legend, throwing one coin into the fountain will ensure a return trip to Rome, two coins will ensure a return trip and a wish granted, and three coins will ensure a return trip, a wish granted, and a future marriage.

The Trevi Fountain is a popular tourist destination and attracts large crowds, especially at night when illuminated. If you're visiting Rome, the Trevi Fountain is a must-see attraction and is a short walk from other popular landmarks, such as the Pantheon and the Spanish Steps.

The Trevi Fountain is a baroque-style fountain located in the heart of Rome, Italy, and is considered a city symbol. Here's a quick guide for visiting the Trevi Fountain:

LOCATION: The Trevi Fountain is located in the historic center of Rome, near Piazza di Trevi.

OPENING HOURS: The Trevi Fountain is open 24 hours a day, seven days a week.

ADMISSION: Admission to the Trevi Fountain is free.

TOUR OPTIONS: Guided tours of the Trevi Fountain and surrounding area are available, which provide a deeper insight into the history and cultural significance of the fountain.

CROWDS: The Trevi Fountain is a popular tourist attraction and can get crowded, especially during peak tourist season.

SAFETY MEASURES: Due to COVID-19, safety measures such as face masks and social distancing are mandatory around the Trevi Fountain.

THROWING COINS: Visitors to the Trevi Fountain are said to have good luck if they throw a coin into the fountain with their right hand over their left shoulder. According to legend, throwing one coin into the fountain will ensure a return trip to Rome, two coins will ensure a return trip and a wish granted, and three coins will ensure a return trip, a wish granted, and a future marriage.

Throw a coin into the Fontana di Trevi, also known as the Trevi Fountain, and according to mythology, you will one day return to the city. However, after visiting Rome, that is already a certainty. Undoubtedly a gorgeous site, but also a chaotic location; you might need to wait in line to snap a picture, but accept this and enjoy the surroundings while you wait.

Visiting the Trevi Fountain is a unique and magical experience. Enjoy your visit!

PIAZZA NAVONA

Piazza Navona is a public square located in Rome, Italy. It is one of the city's most famous and beautiful squares and is known for its three magnificent fountains and elegant baroque architecture.

Piazza Navona was built on the site of an ancient stadium, the Stadium of Domitian, and is considered one of the best examples of baroque architecture in Rome. The square is surrounded by beautiful palaces and is home to three magnificent fountains, each designed by different artists: the Fontana dei Quattro Fiumi, the Fontana del Moro, and the Fontana del Nettuno.

Piazza Navona is a popular gathering place for tourists and locals and is a great place to sit and relax while admiring the beautiful fountains and baroque architecture. It is also a popular spot for street performers, artists, and vendors, who add to the lively atmosphere of the square.

In addition to its fountains, Piazza Navona is also home to several restaurants, cafes, and bars, making it a great place to stop for a meal or a drink. Whether you're interested in history or architecture or want to experience the vibrant atmosphere of one of Rome's most famous squares, Piazza Navona is a must-visit destination.

Piazza Navona is a public square in Rome, Italy, one of the city's most famous and beautiful squares. Here's a quick travel guide for visiting Piazza Navona:

LOCATION: Piazza Navona is in the heart of Rome, near the Pantheon.

OPENING HOURS: Piazza Navona is open 24 hours a day, seven days a week.

ADMISSION: Admission to Piazza Navona is free.

TOUR OPTIONS: Guided tours of Piazza Navona and the surrounding area are available, which provide a deeper insight into the history and cultural significance of the square.

CROWDS: Piazza Navona is a popular tourist attraction and can get crowded, especially during peak tourist season.

SAFETY MEASURES: Due to COVID-19, safety measures such as face masks and social distancing are mandatory in Piazza Navona.

ATTRACTIONS: Piazza Navona is famous for its three magnificent fountains and elegant baroque architecture. It is also a popular spot for street performers, artists, and vendors, who add to the lively atmosphere of the square.

FOOD AND DRINKS: Piazza Navona is home to several restaurants, cafes, and bars, making it a great place to stop for a meal or a drink.

Visiting Piazza Navona is a unique and magical experience. Enjoy your visit!

PANTHEON

Another well-known structure in Rome is the Pantheon, which was constructed as a temple for the deities of Classical Rome. One of the key factors contributing to the Pantheon's popularity as a tourist destination is its dome, which is among the largest in the world and solely illuminated by the oculus (the center of the dome). It is a wonderful site open daily and free to enter; if you'd like a tour, a few euros would do.

The Pantheon is an extremely old building that dates back about 1,800 years. But the building is still standing. The Pantheon, which translates as "temple to all gods," was erected by Emperor Hadrian in 125 AD. The entrance is a whopping 9 meters wide. The only light source in this area is that. Famous figures like Umberto I, Vittorio Emmanuel II, Renaissance artist Raphael, and two Italian Kings are buried here. The structure contains artifacts from numerous cultures. From this, you can learn a lot about Roman culture. You can discover more about their language, clothes, woodwork, sculpture, and other aspects. You can discover what's going through their minds. The Pantheon does not charge admission. Visitors are welcome any day of the week. All holidays, except for Christmas, are closed.

The Pantheon is an ancient temple in Rome, Italy, originally built as a temple to all the gods of ancient Rome. It was constructed between 118 and 128 AD and is considered one of the best-preserved buildings from ancient Rome.

The Pantheon is famous for its unique architectural features, including its massive dome, which has a diameter of 43.3 meters (142 feet) and is still the largest unsupported concrete dome in the world. The interior of the Pantheon is characterized by its circular shape, with a central opening or oculus, which serves as the main source of light for the interior.

In the 7th century, the Pantheon was converted into a Christian church and served as a place of worship. Today, the Pantheon is one of Rome's most popular tourist attractions and is considered a masterpiece of ancient architecture. Visitors can tour the interior of the Pantheon, admire its beautiful marble columns, and learn about its rich history and cultural significance.

The Pantheon is an ancient temple located in Rome, Italy, considered one of the best-preserved buildings from ancient Rome. Here's a quick guide for visiting the Pantheon:

LOCATION: The Pantheon is in the heart of Rome, near Piazza della Rotonda.

OPENING HOURS: It is open daily from 9:00 am to 7:30 pm, with extended hours during the summer.

ADMISSION: Admission to the Pantheon is free.

TOUR OPTIONS: Guided tours of the Pantheon are available, which provide a deeper insight into the history and architecture of the building.

ACCESSIBILITY: The Pantheon is accessible for visitors with mobility limitations, with ramps available for the entrance.

SAFETY MEASURES: Due to COVID-19, safety measures such as face masks and social distancing are mandatory inside the Pantheon.

WHAT TO SEE: The Pantheon is famous for its massive dome, which has a diameter of 43.3 meters (142 feet) and is still the largest unsupported concrete dome in the world. The interior of the Pantheon is characterized by its circular shape, with a central opening or oculus, which serves as the main source of light for the interior.

Visiting the Pantheon is a unique experience that provides a glimpse into the history and culture of ancient Rome. Enjoy your visit!

ROMAN FORUM

The Roman Forum, also known as Foro Romano, should be seen after the Colosseum. Due to its historical significance as the former civic hub of ancient Rome. All key events, political, religious, or otherwise, happened here. Even 2000 years later, its buildings still accurately represent Roman architecture. There is no charge to enter this location, and it is open from nine in the morning to one hour before sunset. Additionally offered are paid audio and guided tours.

The ruins of numerous temples, basilicas, and arches constructed in all Roman towns make up the enormous Roman Fora (one forum, two fora). The forum served as the Roman imperial version of a city's commercial hub; it was where the Senate met and where people also socialized, conducted business, delivered speeches in public, and even received an education.

Its history dates back to five hundred years before Christ, and its primary uses were as a marketplace and gathering spot. Interestingly about the Second Century BC, the Romans decided to clean up their act, banned the prostitutes and the food vendors, and focussed more on the civic part of the events.

The forum's boundaries also included the courthouses. The Curia, or Senate-house, was where public discussions about finance, religion, or business took place. Twenty triumphal arches were thought to have been housed in the fora to match the splendor of Rome, but today only five still stand.

Even though this Roman relic is a tiny fraction of its former size, it still amply illustrates the might and ingenuity of ancient Rome.

The Roman Forum was the center of ancient Rome's political, commercial, and social life. It was a large public square surrounded by important government buildings, temples, and markets and was the site of many important events and ceremonies throughout Roman history.

The House of the Vestals, the Arch of Septimus Severus, the Temple of Saturn, and other ancient Roman ruins can be found at the Roman Forum, a free tourist destination.

Today, the Roman Forum is a popular tourist attraction and a testament to ancient Rome's rich history and cultural heritage. Visitors can explore the remains of several important structures, including the Temple of Saturn, the Temple of Vesta, and the Arch of Titus.

The Roman Forum is located near the Colosseum and can be visited as part of a tour of ancient Rome. Guided tours are available, which provide a deeper insight into the history and significance of the forum.

Visitors to the Roman Forum can also visit the nearby Palatine Hill, which offers stunning views over the City of Rome and was once the location of several important palaces, including the Palace of Augustus.

Whether you're interested in history and architecture or want to experience ancient Rome's beauty and cultural significance, the Roman Forum is a must-visit destination.

The Roman Forum was the center of political, commercial, and social life in ancient Rome and is now a popular tourist attraction. Here's a quick travel guide for visiting the Roman Forum:

LOCATION: The Roman Forum is located in the heart of Rome, near the Colosseum.

OPENING HOURS: The Roman Forum is open from 8:30 am to one hour before sunset, seven days a week.

ADMISSION: Admission to the Roman Forum is included in the ticket to the Colosseum, which also includes entry to Palatine Hill.

TOUR OPTIONS: Guided tours of the Roman Forum are available, which provide a deeper insight into the history and cultural significance of the site.

CROWDS: The Roman Forum can get crowded, especially during peak tourist season.

SAFETY MEASURES: Due to COVID-19, safety measures such as face masks and social distancing are mandatory in the Roman Forum.

ATTRACTIONS: The Roman Forum features the remains of several important structures, including the Temple of Saturn, the Temple of

Vesta, and the Arch of Titus. Visitors can also visit the nearby Palatine Hill.

FOOD AND DRINKS: There is no food or drink facilities within the Roman Forum, but several options are nearby.

Visiting the Roman Forum is a unique and enriching experience. Enjoy your visit!

THE SPANISH STEPS

The 138 steps in the twelve flights that make up the Spanish Steps present a double challenge to the leg muscles because of their various widths. The steps were constructed and given their name to connect the Holy See to the Bourbon Spanish Embassy. In front of the stairs is the well-known Barcaccia fountain, also known as the "ugly boat," which has a sizable boat that spews water as it goes under.

The Spanish Steps are a famous staircase located in Rome, Italy. They connect the Piazza di Spagna to the Church of Trinità dei Monti and are a popular tourist destination. Here's a quick travel guide to help you plan your visit:

LOCATION: The Spanish Steps are located in the heart of Rome, near the Piazza di Spagna and the Trevi Fountain, and they are easily accessible by foot or public transportation.

TIMINGS: The Spanish Steps are open 24 hours a day, seven days a week, and are free to visit.

SURROUNDING ATTRACTIONS: The Spanish Steps are surrounded by many popular attractions, including the Piazza di Spagna, the Trevi Fountain, and the Villa Borghese.

FOOD AND DRINK: There are many cafes and restaurants in the area offering various food and drink options.

Photography is allowed on the Spanish Steps, but be mindful of other visitors and avoid blocking the steps or creating a disturbance.

SAFETY: As with any popular tourist destination, it's important to be aware of pickpockets and other types of crime in the area. Keep your valuables safe and be mindful of your surroundings.

In conclusion, visiting the Spanish Steps is a must-do for anyone visiting Rome. Enjoy the beautiful views and explore the surrounding attractions for a memorable experience.

CIRCUS MAXIMUS.

The Circus Maximus was a historic chariot-racing arena in Rome, Italy, situated in the valley between the Aventine and Palatine hills. With a capacity for 150,000 spectators, it was the biggest arena in antiquity.

Circus Maximus was the site of many important events in ancient Roman history, including religious ceremonies, triumphal processions, and chariot races. These races were a popular form of entertainment in ancient Rome and drew large crowds from all over the city.

Today, the remains of Circus Maximus can still be seen in Rome, but much of the original structure has been destroyed over time. Visitors can walk through the site, which provides a glimpse into ancient Rome's history and cultural significance.

There are no admission fees or opening hours for visiting Circus Maximus, as the site is open to the public and accessible at all times. Visitors are welcome to explore the site independently or join a guided tour for a more in-depth experience.

Visiting Circus Maximus is a unique opportunity to step back in time and experience ancient Rome's history and cultural heritage.

Circus Maximus was an ancient Roman chariot-racing stadium located in Rome, Italy. Here's a quick travel guide for visiting Circus Maximus:

LOCATION: Circus Maximus is in Rome's valley between the Aventine and Palatine hills.

OPENING HOURS: Circus Maximus is open to the public at all times, with no admission fees or opening hours.

TOUR OPTIONS: Guided tours of Circus Maximus are available for those who want a deeper understanding of the site's history and cultural significance.

ACCESSIBILITY: The site of Circus Maximus is open to the public and accessible to visitors of all ages and abilities.

SAFETY MEASURES: Due to COVID-19, measures such as face masks and social distancing may be required in Circus Maximus.

WHAT TO SEE: Visitors to Circus Maximus can see the remains of the ancient chariot-racing stadium, including the starting gates and the track.

FOOD AND DRINKS: Circus Maximus has no food or drink facilities, but several options are nearby.

Visiting Circus Maximus is a unique opportunity to experience ancient Rome's history and cultural significance. Enjoy your visit!

OSTIA ANTICA

While the lives and achievements of the wealthy and famous are widely remembered in museums worldwide, the average person is frequently disregarded, but not here. The museum in Ostia Antica is devoted to remembering the contributions made by the common people to Rome's glory. At the mouth of the Tiber, one of Rome's two rivers, the museum is located in the Ostia neighborhood, which once served as the city's harbor and commercial center. The museum is outstanding, and the remains include a temple, a forum, baths, a theater, and merchants' offices.

Three hundred years before Christ, parts of the region were inhabited. Instead of showing how a Senate or administrative body operates, the exhibitions show how a city functions on a commercial and artisan level. We're all familiar with people like Julius Caesar, whose audacity helped him rise to power and prominence. But what about the man who kept track of this huge city's imports and exports?

Ostia Antica is an ancient Roman city located near Rome, Italy. It was once the main port of Rome and offered a unique glimpse into the daily life of the Roman Empire. Here's a quick travel guide to help you plan your visit:

TIMINGS: Ostia Antica is open every day except Mondays, with extended hours in the summer months. It usually opens at 9:00 am and closes at either 4:00 pm or 7:00 pm, depending on the season.

ADMISSION: Admission to Ostia Antica is by ticket, which can be purchased at the site. Prices vary based on the ticket type, with discounts available for students, seniors, and children.

GUIDED TOURS: Guided tours of Ostia Antica are available and provide a more in-depth understanding of the site and its history.

PHOTOGRAPHY: Photography is allowed in Ostia Antica, but flash photography is not permitted.

ACCESSIBILITY: Some parts of Ostia Antica may be difficult for visitors with disabilities, but the site has taken steps to improve accessibility in recent years.

FOOD AND DRINK: Ostia Antica has no restaurants or cafes, but several options are nearby for food and drink.

In conclusion, visiting Ostia Antica is a unique opportunity to experience ancient Roman life, and planning can help ensure a smooth and enjoyable visit.

THE CATACOMBS

The underground Christian cemetery was known as the Catacombs of Rome. Romans prohibited funerals inside the city walls because they conducted cremation procedures. Because they believed that a corpse needed to be preserved in its entirety for resurrection, early Christians outlawed cremation. Early Christians had no personal property ownership, and the Church did not have enough time to gather enough land collectively to permit individual graves, which was difficult.

Ingenious underground tubes were frequently dug four layers deep after being carved into the walls. The dead might be spread out and shrouded with plenty of room. Rich people had a stone slab over their graves to keep the animals from scavenging their corpses. The death date and even a straightforward Christian sign were frequently engraved on this. Presumably, this is how the current memorial headstone's brief past looked.

Not all the people who were originally buried here had passed away naturally. Many early Christians who died as martyrs were interred here in open graves. The Church had already gained territory, wealth, and power by the fifth century when this tactic was still being used after hundreds of years. After that, the custom was abandoned because it was now possible to bury a person above the earth, if not at ground level. Many of these old ossified bones were taken at the popes' orders during the eighth and ninth centuries when the Goths attacked Rome. This was done to preserve the martyrs' relics, which were revered even at the time. Rome has more than sixty catacombs and hundreds of kilometers of tunnels that have been used for almost 500 years.

Catacombs are underground burial sites, often located in cities, and used to bury the dead in ancient times. Several famous catacombs worldwide, including Rome, Paris, and Alexandria. Here's a quick travel guide for visiting catacombs:

LOCATION: Check for catacombs in the city you visit, and plan for directions and transportation.

TIMINGS: Catacombs typically have set visiting hours and may be closed on certain days of the week, so checking in advance is important.

ADMISSION: Admission is usually by ticket, which can be purchased at the site. Prices vary depending on the location and type of tour.

GUIDED TOURS: Guided tours are often available and provide a more in-depth understanding of the history and significance of the site.

PHOTOGRAPHY: Photography is usually allowed in catacombs, but flash photography is often prohibited.

HEALTH AND SAFETY: Catacombs are often underground, dark, and humid, so it's important to be prepared. Wear comfortable clothing and shoes, and be aware of low ceilings and uneven surfaces.

RESPECT: Catacombs are often sacred sites, so it's important to show respect and follow any rules or guidelines set by the site.

In conclusion, visiting the catacombs is a unique opportunity to learn about ancient burial practices and the city's history. Plan ahead, be respectful and stay safe for a memorable experience.

CHAPTERS 2: MUSEUMS AND ART GALLERIES

Rome is a lovely destination and one of the most romantic cities in the world. One should visit several attractions in Rome, including some of the most well-known architectural marvels, fountains, museums, and art galleries. If this is your first time in Rome, it is advised that you bring this travel guide with you, which will be very helpful. You can be confident that you won't get lost in Rome because the guide will provide you with all the precise directions and information you need.

Rome has many top attractions. A few historic monuments, Renaissance and medieval buildings, fountains, and sizable museums may all be found in Rome.

Rome is essentially an outdoor museum, a city that has maintained a noticeable architectural homogeneity and has undergone little industrialization or modernization. No wonder you may spend the day exploring the temples, squares, shops, bell towers, and other sites that will leave a lasting impression on tourists.

The city grew steadily and shone thanks brilliantly to theaters, temples, and baths situated close to magnificent structures, which led to the fall of such a mighty empire. Rome became Christian, and Renaissance and Baroque art were displayed across the city.

Rome is home to many world-renowned museums and art galleries, showcasing the city's rich history and cultural heritage. Here are some of the most famous museums and art galleries in Rome:

VATICAN MUSEUMS: The Vatican Museums are a complex of museums and galleries located within Vatican City. They house one of the world's largest collections of art and artifacts, including the Sistine Chapel and the Raphael Rooms.

CAPITOLINE MUSEUMS: The Capitoline Museums are located on Capitoline Hill in Rome and contain a vast collection of art, sculptures, and ancient artifacts.

GALLERIA BORGHESE: The Galleria Borghese is a stunning art gallery in the Villa Borghese park in Rome. It houses a magnificent collection of works by Bernini, Canova, Caravaggio, and other great artists.

NATIONAL ROMAN MUSEUM: The National Roman Museum is a complex of museums located in various sites throughout Rome, including the Palazzo Massimo and the Baths of Diocletian. It contains a vast collection of artifacts and artworks from ancient Rome.

MACRO MUSEUM: The MACRO Museum is a modern and contemporary art museum located in the Testaccio neighborhood of Rome. It features exhibitions by both established and emerging artists.

MAXXI MUSEUM: The Maxxi Museum is a contemporary art museum located in the Flaminio neighborhood of Rome. It features exhibitions of contemporary art, architecture, and design.

These are just a few of Rome's museums and art galleries that are well worth visiting. Whether you're interested in ancient art, modern masterpieces, or contemporary creations, Rome has something for everyone.

Why not visit the Pasta Museum, one of Rome's most laid-back sights, if you still have some time? Every day of the week, the museum is open, and admission is roughly 10 euros per person.

Classic Italian art may be seen in numerous museums, and day journeys to less visited but no less beautiful regions of Italy, such as Assisi, Palestrina, and Frascati, are simple to arrange by train services or coach tours.

NATIONAL ROMAN MUSEUM

The National Roman Museum (Museo Nazionale Romano) is a collection of museums in Rome, Italy, dedicated to studying and preserving ancient Roman art, culture, and history. It comprises several branches, including the Palazzo Massimo alle Terme, the Baths of Diocletian, the Crypta Balbi, and the Palazzo Altemps. The collections include sculptures, frescoes, mosaics, coins, and other artifacts that provide insight into ancient Rome's daily life, beliefs, and artistic traditions. The museum is considered one of the world's largest and most important collections of Roman art and artifacts.

Here is a brief travel guide for visiting the National Roman Museum:

LOCATION: The museum is in Rome, Italy and has several branches, including the Palazzo Massimo alle Terme, the Baths of Diocletian, the Crypta Balbi, and the Palazzo Altemps.

OPENING HOURS: The opening hours for the museum branches vary, but most are open from 9:00 am to 7:30 pm

THE BORGHESE GALLERY

The Borghese Gallery (Galleria Borghese) is an art museum in Rome, Italy. It is housed in the Villa Borghese park and is considered one of the most important museums in the world for its collection of Renaissance and Baroque masterpieces.

The Borghese Gallery features works by famous artists, including Bernini, Canova, Caravaggio, and Raphael. The collection includes sculptures, paintings, frescoes, drawings, and ancient Roman and Greek sculptures and artifacts.

Visitors must reserve tickets in advance, as the number of visitors allowed in the gallery at any given time is limited. The museum is closed on Mondays, and visitors are asked to adhere to a dress code requiring covered shoulders and no shorts or miniskirts.

If you're an art lover, the Borghese Gallery is a must-see destination in Rome, offering an impressive collection of masterpieces in a beautiful setting.

Numerous museums and galleries are located in the calming, English-style gardens of Villa Borghese, where you may combine culture with the serenity of the landscaped grounds. Bring a picnic and take in a leisurely Roman afternoon in the summer.

Here is a brief travel guide for visiting the Borghese Gallery:

LOCATION: The Borghese Gallery is located in the Villa Borghese park in Rome, Italy.

OPENING HOURS: The gallery is open from Tuesday to Sunday from 9:00 am to 7:00 pm and is closed on Mondays.

ADMISSION: Reservation is required to visit the Borghese Gallery. Visitors are limited to a maximum of three hours inside the gallery.

DRESS CODE: Visitors are asked to adhere to a dress code requiring covered shoulders and no shorts or miniskirts.

ACCESSIBILITY: The Borghese Gallery is partially accessible to visitors with disabilities.

NEARBY ATTRACTIONS: The Villa Borghese park is a large public park in Rome and is home to several other museums, including the Galleria Nazionale d'Arte Moderna, the Bioparco di Roma, and the Museo Etrusco di Villa Giulia.

Note: To avoid long lines and ensure an optimal experience, it's recommended to book tickets in advance.

THE NATIONAL GALLERY OF ANCIENT ART.

The National Gallery of Ancient Art (Galleria Nazionale d'Arte Antica) is an art museum in Rome, Italy. It is dedicated to preserving and displaying Italian paintings from the 13th to the 18th centuries.

The museum's collection includes works by some of the most famous Italian artists of the Renaissance and Baroque periods, including Caravaggio, Raphael, Tintoretto, and Titian. The gallery also features a large collection of ancient sculptures and decorative arts, including tapestries, ceramics, and furnishings.

The National Gallery of Ancient Art is housed in the Palazzo Barberini, a 17th-century palace in the heart of Rome. The palace is famous for its ornate frescoes and stucco work, making it a beautiful setting for the museum's collection.

Visitors to the National Gallery of Ancient Art can expect a diverse and extensive collection of Italian art and artifacts in a beautiful historic setting.

Here is a brief travel guide for visiting the National Gallery of Ancient Art:

LOCATION: The National Gallery of Ancient Art is located in the Palazzo Barberini in Rome, Italy.

OPENING HOURS: The museum is open from Tuesday to Sunday from 8:30 am to 7:30 pm and is closed on Mondays.

ADMISSION: Admission to the museum is free for EU citizens under 18 and over 65 and EU teachers. All other visitors can purchase tickets at the museum or online in advance.

ACCESSIBILITY: The National Gallery of Ancient Art is partially accessible to visitors with disabilities.

NEARBY ATTRACTIONS: The Palazzo Barberini is located near several other historic landmarks and museums in Rome, including the Trevi Fountain, the Spanish Steps, and the Villa Borghese park.

NOTE: To avoid long lines and ensure an optimal experience, it's recommended to book tickets in advance or visit early in the morning or late in the afternoon.

CHAPTERS 3: CUISINE AND WINE

Rome is famous for its cuisine; many restaurants and cafes serve traditional Italian dishes and local wines. There are cafes and restaurants virtually everywhere in Rome, so locating one when you're hungry won't be a problem. The dress and shoes should be comfortable for travel and limit the amount of luggage you bring.

Rome, the capital city of Italy, is renowned for its rich and diverse cuisine. The city's culinary traditions are rooted in its history, with dishes passed down for generations and ingredients grown locally or sourced from the surrounding countryside. The oldest ice cream business and well-known café in Rome, Italy, is called Giolitti, and in 1890, it was founded.

Traditional Roman dishes include:

- Carciofi alla giudia: deep-fried artichokes
- Saltimbocca alla romana: veal with prosciutto and sage
- Cacio e pepe: pasta with cheese and black pepper
- Supplì: fried rice balls with mozzarella cheese and tomato sauce
- Bucatini all'amatriciana: pasta with tomato sauce, bacon, and pecorino cheese

Rome is also known for its wine, particularly its red wines, such as the well-regarded Frascati and Est! Est!! Est!!! Wines from the nearby

Castelli Romani hills. White wines from the area, including the Greco di Tufo and the Fiano di Avellino, are also popular.

Visitors to Rome can enjoy its cuisine in traditional trattorias and pizzerias, as well as in more upscale restaurants. The city's food markets, such as the Campo de' Fiori market, offer a chance to sample fresh local ingredients and traditional dishes.

TYPICAL DISHES

Rome, Italy, is known for its rich and flavorful cuisine steeped in history and tradition. Here are some of the city's most popular and typical dishes:

Cacio e Pepe: A simple pasta dish made with spaghetti, Pecorino Romano cheese, and black pepper. The name of one of the most well-known pasta dishes in the city, cacio e pepe, answers: "cacio" is the neighbourhood term for Pecorino Romano, a salty, aged sheep's milk cheese, and "pepe" is black pepper.

To make a smooth sauce, the two ingredients are blended with cooked pasta and a little of its cooking water. Salumeria Roscioli has a fantastic rendition, while Cesare al Casaletto is noted for its looser, more liquid take on the traditional dish.

Carbonara: A pasta dish with eggs, pancetta or guanciale, Pecorino Romano cheese, and black pepper. In Rome, many meals are the subject of fierce discussion, with carbonara being the most heated.

Every cook and diner has very strong ideas about where the food came from and what goes into it, and they are completely unyielding when faced with modifications. However, there is one issue about which all Italians can agree: cream should never be put to carbonara.

In general, pecorino romano or a blend of pecorino romano and Parmigiano-Reggiano, black pepper, spaghetti or rigatoni, guanciale or pancetta, egg yolk or a whole egg, are the ingredients used to make the dish. The sauce is thickened by slowly heating the eggs, which should adhere to the pasta for a smooth, non-scrambled appearance.

Saltimbocca alla Romana: Veal escalopes topped with prosciutto and sage, usually sautéed in butter or olive oil.

Supplì: Fried rice balls filled with mozzarella cheese and tomato sauce. Rice croquettes are a common side dish at pizzerias and takeaways in Rome. The traditional recipe calls for rice and tomato sauce to be cooked together until the mixture is thick and creamy, along with chunks of ground meat, sausage, or chicken gizzards (or all of the above!). After cooling, the rice is fashioned into egg-shaped parcels wrapped around a slice of mozzarella, breaded, and deep-fried. When broken open, the finished supply ought to expose melted mozzarella.

The traditional tomato and meat sauce recipe dates back to the early 20th century. Still, today's inventive chefs are flavouring the rice with modern ingredients like Pecorino and black pepper or radicchio and gorgonzola. For both the traditional and modern versions, visit Supplizio, Pizzarium, and Trapizzino.

Carciofi alla Giudia: Deep-fried artichokes seasoned with salt, lemon, and olive oil. Carciofi alla giudia (Jewish-style fried artichokes), a dish made from this flavorful thistle, is on every foodie traveller's must-try list. Artichokes are available year-round at markets and served in restaurants due to demand from both visitors and locals.

Visit Rome during the winter months when it is in the season to sample the renowned native globe artichoke or carciofo romanesco. In addition to the well-known fried dish popular in the Ghetto, Rome's old Jewish neighbourhood, you can get carciofi alla romana, or artichokes cooked in oil and herbs, on nearly every menu.

Ossobuco alla Romana: A hearty stew made with cross-cut veal shanks, tomatoes, celery, carrot, and white wine.

Gricia: A pasta dish made with pancetta, Pecorino Romano cheese, and black pepper.

Porchetta meat served with bread: Porchetta is a roasted pig that has been deboned. Despite possible variations in the specific cuts, belly and loin are frequently prepared with salt, pepper, and herbs. A great specimen of porchetta can be difficult to find, even though it is very common and can be found at delis and takeaway restaurants as a sandwich filling.

Visit Panificio Bonci, close to the Vatican, and get slices of pork sandwiched between crispy pieces of pizza bianca, the basic regional flatbread, for a genuinely excellent, moist, and perfectly seasoned porchetta experience.

Pizza al taglio: A pizza sold by the slice and often served as street food. In Rome, the term "pizza" is used to describe a variety of flatbreads and round personal pizzas. In the distinctively Roman pizza type, pizza al taglio (pizza by the slice), the dough is either ornamented and baked in sheet pans or shaped into an oblong shape.

The pizza is always served by the slice and is divided into the guests' preferred portions with a knife or pair of scissors. The way the pizza is served varies from establishment to establishment, but it's always done casually without any table service or frills.

Gnocchi alla romana: Small, semolina-based dumplings, typically served with tomato sauce, melted butter, and Parmesan cheese.

These dishes are just a few examples of the delicious and diverse cuisine that Rome has to offer. Whether you're looking for a quick and hearty snack or a multi-course feast, you're sure to find something that satisfies your appetite in this historic city.

Allesso di Bollito(Bread roll with meat and spinach): When butchers invented slow-cooked techniques to soften tough cuts of beef, stewed beef meals were once very popular in Rome. Some of those classic dishes are no longer popular because the meat is considerably more economical than it once was.

Allesso di bollito, or simmering beef, is very much alive at Mordi E Vai in the Testaccio Market. One of the city's most deliciously resurrected classics, the stand serves soft beef on bread coated in the meat's savory fluids.

Gelato: Numerous gelateria selling traditional flavours and imaginative originals may be found throughout Rome. It should come as no surprise that many locals regularly enjoy this frozen treat, given the abundance of gelato available on their way to work or home.

While there is no doubt a wide variety of irresistible gelato available, few establishments use only natural ingredients. To see this, glance at the ingredients list displayed in most establishments; you'll be surprised by how many vegetable oils, artificial colours, and other junk are present. Instead, stick to establishments like Otaleg, Fatamorgana, and Fior di Luna.

Cream-topped Maritozzi sponge cakes: These days, the cornetto, a mass-produced, margarine-based imitation croissant, is Rome's preferred breakfast pastry. But maritozzi was in charge in the past. These sweet, leavened buns are cut open and filled with whipped cream that has barely been sweetened.

Maritozzi is placed at the entrance of Regoli, a traditional bakery next to Piazza Vittorio, and is piled high with whipped cream. Be warned: there is no elegant way to consume these cream-filled sweets.

Rome boomerang - trapizzino

Stefano Callegari, a renowned experimental pizza maker in Rome, created the trapizzino in 2009. The inventive baker created thick, triangular pizza wedges, cut them open, and stuffed them with traditional Roman fares like meatballs, tongue-in-green sauce, and chicken cacciatore.

There are currently seven Trapizzino locations across the city, with additional locations in Milan, Florence, and New York City, thanks to the creative street food that combined Rome's love of pizza with its love of savoury foods.

LOCAL WINES

Rome's home region of Lazio produces a good number of wines. However, it isn't as well recognized for them as other Italian regions like Tuscany and Abruzzo.

The Lazio region experienced malaria-infested soil in the 1930s. Mussolini implemented a "bonification" program to make the area useable, which required northern workers to bring down local grapes like Merlot or Cabernet. As a result, the region now has a diverse wine sector.

Most of the wine produced in Lazio is white, with Est Est Est from Lake Bolsena, further north toward Umbria, and Frascati from the Castelli Wine Region near Rome being the most well-known examples. Red wine aficionados, take a drink of Cesanese del Piglio or watch the Red Cremere (produced by local vineyard Terre del Veio). There is even rosé wine called Rosato Risona, which is nothing like the sugary, syrupy wine that youngsters drank at the height of elegance in the 1970s.

SYSTEM OF CLASSIFYING WINE

How do you tell if the wine you are buying is a good deal or something that would taste better on your chips? Fortunately, Italy has its system for grading wine excellence. Bring this (not very serious) guide with you, and you won't ever be concerned again.

The abbreviation for controlled and guaranteed origin is DOCG.

Few Italian wines are given this grade, representing the greatest quality acknowledgement. It should be served on important occasions, such as marriage proposals and honeymoons, and be drunk carefully without using a straw. It can also be tasted freely and without restraint at wine tastings.

Denominazione di Origine Controllata (DOC) wine

Nice thing. A wine that has passed a rigorous set of tests to guarantee both its authenticity and the distinctiveness of the region's produce. Most likely, one to purchase for a first date or business lunch, making sure the label is always visible.

Geographic indication, abbreviated as IGT

General table wines that are acceptable. These wines are frequently produced in designated geographical wine-growing areas but without the exacting standards of DOC wines. Excellent DOC wines fall under this category to avoid the paperwork for DOC certification, although they tend to be of lower quality. (It's worthwhile to try them all to make sure.) Works nicely when consumed as a second or third bottle.

Vino Da Tavola, or VdT

This designates wines that only meet the requirement that they were made in Italy. Fine in an emergency, but best suited for buying as a gift to family or coworkers you don't particularly care for.

Ask for the house wine, or "vino sfuso," which is inexpensive (you should pay about €4 for half a litre) and goes down easily if all of that sounds too much trouble. The greatest recommendation is to give them all a try!

Rome, Italy, is located in the Lazio region, known for its wine production. Some of the local wines that are produced in the area around Rome include:

Frascati: A white wine made from Malvasia and Trebbiano grapes, Frascati is one of the oldest and most well-known wines from the Lazio region.

Est! Est!! Est!!!: A dry white wine made from the Trebbiano grape, Est! Est!! Est!!! It is named after a medieval legend about a bishop who marked his favourite wines along the way with the Latin phrase "Est! Est!! Est!!!".

Castelli Romani Rosso: A red wine made from a blend of local grape varieties, including Cesanese, Montepulciano, and Sangiovese.

Greco di Tufo: A white wine made from the Greco grape, grown in the Tufo area near Avellino in the Campania region.

Fiano di Avellino: A white wine made from the Fiano grape, grown in the Avellino area in the Campania region.

These wines are a good representation of the range of styles and flavours that are produced in the Lazio region. Whether you're a seasoned wine connoisseur or just looking to sample something new, you're sure to find a local wine that suits your taste in Rome.

WINE BARS IN ROME

Nothing beats the feeling of unwinding with a glass of wine in the Eternal City after a long day of sightseeing and allowing the vibrant chatter of Romans chewing the fat of the day to wash over you. Wine is loved in Italy with a devotion that borders on religious fervour, and each neighbourhood offers some fantastic spots to savour the fermented delicacies of the noble grape. These establishments, known as enoteche in Italian, frequently offer incredibly long wine lists with producers from around the Italian peninsula and beyond. Always feel free to ask for advice or recommendations, and don't be afraid to be daring and try something new. If you want to make a night of it, you won't go hungry either because many enoteche put up fantastic food pairings to go with your drink.

Now that your appetite has been whetted, check out this list of 10 fantastic establishments in the Eternal City where you may sip fine wines while mingling with locals! In our opinion, these are some of the top wine bars in Rome.

1. ENOTECA IL PICCOLO CENTRO STORICO

The legendary Il Piccolo is the place to grab an early-evening glass and participate in a spot of top-notch people watching under the shadow of Pasquino, Rome's famed speaking statue. It is situated on one of the most atmospheric streets in the centre of Storico, a short hop from Piazza Navona. Small in name and character, the chairs outside Il Piccolo that flow out onto the street are constantly crowded with locals, where old-timers disputing politics and cuisine (this is Italy, after all) brush shoulders with the hiply-dressed centre residents. Prices start at €4 for a large glass, which is more than fair.

2. EMIDIO MOLINARI AND HIS BROTHER FIUME

Enoteca Molinari is a little wine shop in the affluent Fiume neighbourhood, next to the MACRO Museum of Contemporary Art. The walls are lined with dusty shelves stacked high with intriguing bottles and labels, some dating back to the 1920s. Emidio started his wine shop in Rome in 1964 after moving there from Molise, and it has been there ever since. Today, his son Antonio is in charge. He and his daughter Veronica never seem to get tired of giving out helpful recommendations while pouring endless drinks to the thirsty locals who throng the street outside and balance their glasses in increasingly risky positions on conveniently parked scooters and cars. With a glass of Molinari costing only €2.50, it's no surprise that students from the nearby LUISS University enjoy it. With an overwhelming selection of fine wines by the bottle, Molinari still has you covered if you're looking for something with a little more pedigree.

3. CHOURMO CERTOSA PIGNETO.

Chourmo is the neighbourhood pub you've always imagined, located only a few doors down from the famous Roman trattoria Betty e Mary in the lovely neighbourhood of Certosa, east of Pigneto. No frills, simply welcoming proprietors (likely the always endearing Salvatore will become your new best friend), a varied local clientele, excellent Italian wines by the glass for reasonable prices, and frequent free jazz performances on the weekends. What else is there to ask for? The similarly excellent wine bar/bookshop Shakespeare&Co. is right over the street if you want to stay out late.

4. THE CAMPO DE'FIORI VINAIETTO

Forget about the tourist traps with their hawkers and deals that line the historic Campo de Fiori. Go across the block to the old Il Vinaietto on Via del Monte della Farina to experience one of central Rome's most evocative neighbourhoods in its natural state. This always-bustling vineria is crowded with locals, and their exuberant discussion spills onto the street as the place fills up after work. No wifi or smart-working is going on here. The cost of a large glass is only about $3 or $4, but the people-watching is priceless. To enjoy the exciting street theatre of Rome, get a drink inside the tiny shop, which is filled with an odd assortment of memorabilia, such as posters from the Italian

Communist Party and creaking shelves full of bottles. At its most vivid and colourful, the Eternal City.

5. SAN LORENZO'S SORI

Il Sori is a genuinely chic wine bar with unquestionable oenophilic credentials, defying bustling San Lorenzo's reputation for dingy pubs and extremely budget-friendly student hangouts. Il Sor was founded after owner Pasquale decided to start a wine bar after realizing that his home had essentially become a cantina to support his love. Il Sori offers a sizable and intensely individualized selection of wines by the glass and bottle, which is truly a labour of love. Oh, and the food selections are also excellent; traditional small plates to go with your selections include everything from platters of cured meats, cheeses, and olives sourced from small-batch producers all over the peninsula to more elaborate dishes like polpo a la gallega (octopus and potatoes) and steak tartare.

6. AI TRE SCALINI MONTI.

Bohemian Ai Tre Scalini, a landmark in the trendy Monti neighbourhood, has served thirsty travellers drinks since 1895. Ai Tre Scalini's evocative atmosphere makes you feel the weight of history. Still, the hip young population frequents the establishment is drawn by the moderately priced wines available by the glass and carafe. You'll know you've found the right area when you see the lovely creeping vines that snake their way over the street at the corner of Via

Panisperna. If you can't obtain a table here, don't worry; just across the street is the Barzilai, a Roman measure of wine equal to 2 litres, named for a politician famous for serving such enormous carafes of wine to potential voters.

7. THE GOCCETTO HISTORICAL CENTER

The epitome of everything that makes downtown Rome so great is perhaps the ultra-chic il Goccetto (literally "small drop," although chances are you'll be having a lot more than that if you stop in"). Il Goccetto has been operating since 1983 and is housed in a beautiful palazzo designed by 16th-century renowned architect Antonio di Sangallo back in 1527, only steps from the Tiber. A chalkboard lists the more than 20 options by the glass, which change daily. The stunning décor combines modern art and 17th-century details. You may choose from about 1,000 different bottles, so you're sure to find the ideal wine here. Food consists of tiny plates, including Stella from Gaeta, Caprese salad with oven-dried tomatoes, and fish cured with beetroot.

8. TIZIANA CIAMPETTI ESQUILINO'S WINE ART

This little, unassuming establishment in Rome's Esquilino neighbourhood to the south of Termini Station fully fulfils its promise to elevate wine tasting to an art form. It is an invaluable resource for wine lovers of all stripes. In addition to being a formidable source of information on all things wine, the hostess in question, Tiziana, is also extraordinarily friendly. This wine shop is incredibly well-stocked despite its modest size, with a wide variety of lesser-known smaller wineries on its crowded shelves. There are a few tables outdoors, so pull up a stool, ask Tiziana to assist you in choosing a glass and some focaccia, and take in the sights in the lovely light of a Roman evening.

9. IL TIASO ENOLIBRERIA PIGNETO.

On the turbulent seas of Pigneto's lively nightlife scene, ultra-sophisticated Tiaso is a haven of peace. Since opening its doors in 2001, this classy wine bar has witnessed a nearly unrecognizably rapid shift in Pigneto. The fabled court of Dionysius, where the ancient Greek gods indulged in copious amounts of wine, dancing, and musical entertainment, is whence Tiaso derives its name. Tiaso is a dependable neighbourhood fixture that more than lives up to its name. It is crammed to the rafters with tipples from all over Italy offered by the glass or bottle, from budget-friendly local labels to the titans of Italian winemaking. If lucky, you could enjoy live music from the upper balcony in the casual and welcoming ambience. To the next 20 years, cheers!

10. LITRO MONTEVERDE

Litro is unquestionably something you should look into if you're looking for something a little hipper. This contemporary wine bar, located in lush Monteverde and just a short distance from the enormous Villa Doria Pamphili, starkly contrasts the traditional enoteches that have dominated our list. The wine list at Litro reflects its pan-European credentials, specializing in sulphite-free natural and biodynamic wines from small producers across the continent. Litro is bright and airy with an eccentric design that makes it appear more Montmarte than Monteverde. Litro should be your first trip to the Eternal City if you are a natural wine enthusiast.

Additionally, they have a sizable cocktail menu, with mezcal being one of their specialities.

RECOMMENDED RESTAURANTS

Rome, Italy, is home to a diverse and vibrant culinary scene, with a wide range of restaurants serving traditional and contemporary dishes. Here are some highly recommended restaurants in the city:

Trattoria Da Enzo al 29: A traditional trattoria that serves classic Roman dishes in a cozy and charming atmosphere.

Roscioli: A popular restaurant and wine bar that serves traditional Italian cuisine and offers an extensive wine list.

Osteria del Pegno: A chic and modern restaurant serving contemporary Italian cuisine, focusing on seasonal ingredients and traditional techniques.

La Montecarlo: A traditional trattoria that serves classic Roman dishes, including pasta carbonara and saltimbocca alla Romana.

L'Asino d'Oro: A rustic and casual restaurant serving innovative and contemporary Italian cuisine, focusing on locally sourced ingredients.

Pizzeria La Montecarlo: A bustling pizzeria that serves some of the best pizza in Rome, with a focus on using high-quality ingredients and traditional techniques

CHAPTERS 4: ACTIVITIES AND ENTERTAINMENT

Rome, Italy, is rich in history, art, culture, and entertainment. Vatican Museums and Sistine Chapel are a must-see destination for art lovers; the Vatican Museums house some of the world's most famous works of art, including the Sistine Chapel. The iconic symbol of Rome, the Colosseum is a former gladiatorial arena that is now a popular tourist destination.

Roman Forum and Palatine Hill offer a glimpse into ancient Rome's political, social, and commercial center.

One of the best-preserved ancient buildings in Rome, the Pantheon is a former temple that has been transformed into a church.

A beautiful baroque square in the heart of Rome, Piazza Navona is surrounded by restaurants, cafes, and street performers.

A charming neighborhood on the west bank of the Tiber River, Trastevere is known for its narrow streets, historic buildings, and lively nightlife.

Rome, Italy, offers various activities and entertainment options for visitors of all interests. Here are some of the most popular things to do in the city:

Shopping: Rome is home to various shopping options, from high-end designer boutiques to local markets selling handmade goods.

Entertainment: Rome has a thriving entertainment scene, with theatres, cinemas, and music venues offering various performances and events.

Sports: Rome is a sports-loving city, and there are many opportunities to watch or participate in soccer, rugby, basketball, and other sports.

One of the most well-liked tourist destinations in Europe is Rome. Great sights and activities may be found in that old city. Here, the art comes in a variety of powerful, interesting styles. Rome is also the most significant city in western antiquity and the birthplace of European civilization, where the past and present coexist.

Travelers fall in love with Rome because of its distinctive characteristics, including the spectacular thrill of its many years of stormy history, natural occurrences, and architectural gems created by the greatest historical artists.

Travelers seeking art, history, culture, romance, and entertainment should head to Rome. Rome shines at you from every direction, day and night, with a luminous contentment that is pure self-wonder at the astounding depth of knowledge and wisdom it offers. It truly is a 24-hour city, with theaters, restaurants, and pubs just waiting to be discovered at night and museums, galleries, and monuments that can be seen during the day.

Walk through the bustling Italian neighborhood of Trastevere, where there are many places to shop, eat, and drink. Here, you may get away from the crowds of tourists and spend some time observing the residents going about their daily lives. Here, you don't need to have a plan; use your feet to navigate the numerous winding streets and squares.

Rome is home to the Vatican City, which serves as the Pope's residence. It's a unique experience to travel to this tiny landlocked independent state. If you want to roam around the Vatican, it's vital to take something to cover your shoulders as a symbol of respect. It is a worthwhile adventure and simple to get from the center of Rome, thanks to the little stores that line the neighborhood's peripheral streets. While there, see St. Peter's Basilica, the Sistine Chapel, and Michelangelo's painted ceiling. You might even send a postcard to receive the Vatican's postmark.

SHOPPING

Rome, Italy, is a shopper's paradise, offering a wide range of shopping options for visitors of all tastes and budgets. Here are some of the best places to go shopping in the city:

Via del Corso: A busy and historic street in the center of Rome, Via del Corso is lined with shops, boutiques, and department stores.

Via dei Condotti: A luxurious shopping street in the heart of Rome, Via dei Condotti is home to many of the world's top designer boutiques and high-end shops.

Porta Portese Flea Market: One of the largest flea markets in Europe, Porta Portese is a great place to find vintage clothing, antiques, and other unique items.

Campo de' Fiori: A popular square in the heart of Rome, Campo de Fiori is surrounded by shops selling handmade goods, jewelry, and souvenirs.

Il Centro Commerciale Roma Est: One of the largest shopping malls in Rome, Roma Est is a modern and convenient shopping destination offering a wide range of stores and services, including clothing and fashion, electronics, and household goods. With its spacious and air-conditioned environment, it's a great place to escape the heat and crowds of the city centre and offers a convenient and hassle-free shopping experience.

MARKETS

Rome, Italy, is home to various markets, each offering a unique shopping experience and showcasing the city's diverse and vibrant culture. Here are some of the most popular markets in the city:

Campo de' Fiori: A colourful and lively open-air market in the heart of Rome, Campo de' Fiori is a popular destination for fresh produce, flowers, and souvenirs.

Mercato Centrale: A large indoor market in the heart of Rome, Mercato Centrale offers a wide range of products, including fresh produce, meat, cheese, and bakery items.

Porta Portese: A bustling flea market in the Trastevere neighborhood of Rome, Porta Portese is a popular destination for secondhand goods, vintage clothing, and antiques.

Mercato di Testaccio: A lively food market in the Testaccio neighborhood of Rome, Mercato di Testaccio is known for its high-quality ingredients, artisanal products, and street food stalls.

Mercato Monti: A chic and contemporary market in the heart of Rome, Mercato Monti is a hub for local designers, artists, and craftsmen selling handmade goods, jewelry, and clothing.

Piazza di San Cosimato: A charming open-air market in the Trastevere neighborhood of Rome, Piazza di San Cosimato is a great place to sample local foods, buy fresh produce, and browse for souvenirs.

WALKS ALONG THE TIBER, AND PARKS AND GARDENS

Rome, Italy, offers a variety of scenic walks, parks, and gardens for visitors to enjoy. Here are some of the most popular outdoor destinations along the Tiber River and in the city's parks and gardens:

Walks along the Tiber River: The Tiber River runs through the heart of Rome, and the riverbank provides a scenic and peaceful walkway with views of the city's bridges and historic landmarks.

Villa Borghese: One of Rome's largest and most beautiful parks, Villa Borghese is home to the Borghese Gallery, a lake, gardens, and a zoo.

Villa Ada: A large park in the north of Rome, Villa Ada is a popular destination for picnics, jogging, and nature walks.

Villa Doria Pamphilj: A vast park on the outskirts of Rome, Villa Doria Pamphilj is known for its beautiful gardens, rolling hills, and scenic views of the city.

Giardino degli Aranci: A small park on the Aventine Hill in Rome, Giardino degli Aranci offers stunning views of the city and a peaceful oasis in the heart of the city.

These outdoor destinations offer a chance to escape the crowds, relax in nature, and enjoy the beauty of Rome.

CHAPTER 5: WALKING ITINERARIES

Rome planning is one of the most challenging tasks, and planning the complete itinerary is the best approach to preparing for Rome.

PRACTICAL ROME TRAVEL TIPS

Here are a few fast, practical city travel tips. To enter Italy, you must have a valid passport, but if your stay is less than 90 days, you do not require a visa. For a few particular nations, there is an exception to this rule. It would help if you travelled to Rome between October and March because summers are hot and dry. Make reservations at a hotel close to the historic area. The perfect place would be Hotel de Russie, between the Piazza del Popolo and the Spanish Steps, which are worth viewing.

Plan your plan well in advance, paying particular attention to the locations you must see. Walking allows you to explore the sites at your own pace, making it the best way to learn about Rome's history. Utilizing the Tram Bus system, which connects the entire city and its environs, is another cost-effective option.

Additionally, you can always choose a private tour if convenience is important. Make sure you have a pair of cosy shoes with you. Carry as little as possible when moving about the city. You may satisfy your appetite anytime because the city has a lot of eateries close to popular tourist destinations.

There are so many tourist sites in the city that choosing which ones to see is difficult. This could be your itinerary for a day of local touring. Start with the Coliseum, a well-liked tourist destination. Verify the times in advance because the visitation hours fluctuate throughout the year. They offer an hourly guided tour led by tour guides dressed as gladiators to make this wonderful experience more realistic. Foro Romano, the next significant station, is located directly across the street. Even after 2000 years, the Roman Forum, the Roman Empire's centre, is still strong! You would find the changes in Roman architecture fascinating. There is no entrance cost, and you can choose the guided tour option.

The Pantheon, also known as "The Temple to All Gods," is the next visit and one of Rome's best-preserved structures. It was constructed around 125 AD. Many well-known people are buried here, including the only Raphael and the Italian kings Vittorio Emmanuel II and Umberto I.

The Roman Emperor Hadrian built this structure. This monument's only light source comes from a nine-meter aperture in the concrete dome. It transports you back to the heyday of the Roman Empire, and you can't help but fantasize about living in Rome at that time. You would have goosebumps as you imagined the attire, language, gestures, etc., that they would have used. Throughout the year, except for Christmas, when the Pantheon is closed, you can enjoy this extraordinary experience.

In the end, there is only one more location to visit that must be done. The Vatican's large collection of historical items can easily keep you busy for three hours. Allow Michelangelo's Pieta, which is kept in St. Peter's Basilica, to astound you if you have the time. Egyptian mummies are among the magnificent antiquities that may be found in the Vatican museum. You must visit the Sistine Chapel, where Michelangelo painted The Bible on the ceiling.

Whatever you decide to do, make friends with the hotel concierge first because he can be your finest source for current information.

LOCATIONS TO VISIT

Rome is a captivating location that draws visitors because of its extensive cultural history and magnificent ancient landmarks. In the 2004 Readers' Choice Awards for Condé Nast Traveler, Rome earned second place among the top ten European cities.

Rome, Italy, is rich in history, art, and culture, making it an ideal destination for walking tours. Here are some of the most popular walking itineraries for exploring the city:

The Vatican and St. Peter's Basilica: This walking tour takes you through Vatican City, where you can see St. Peter's Square, the Vatican Museums, and the Sistine Chapel, as well as the magnificent St. Peter's Basilica.

The Colosseum and Ancient Rome: This walking tour takes you through the heart of Ancient Rome, where you can see the Colosseum, the Roman Forum, and Palatine Hill.

Baroque Rome: This walking tour takes you through the streets of Baroque Rome, where you can see the magnificent bar

All of the locations in Rome on the list are accessible in a single day, and you can spend the next three hours in the Vatican. Huge collections of books, artwork, sculptures, and other items about the history of the Catholic Church can be found here.

However, there are too many pieces to explore in this short time. The Vatican collection cannot be completely browsed in one sitting, and you may view Michelangelo's Pieta in St. Peter's. The majestic Vatican Museum is another option; it houses some outstanding antiquities.

Mummies from Egypt can be found here as well. The Sistine Chapel is one location that you absolutely must see, though. The Bible was painted on the Sistine Chapel ceiling by Michelangelo, a great sculptor who was hired by Pope Julius II. His attempt to humiliate Michelangelo was unsuccessful, however, as the Sistine Chapel went on to rank among the greatest works of art produced during the Renaissance. It would help if you made inquiries well in advance because the schedules around here aren't very consistent.

There are several tourist traps in and around Rome, including the Colosseum, the Trevi Fountain (where it is said that if you throw two pennies in, you will discover your true love), the Spanish Steps, and the Pantheon. The Metro underground system and numerous buses make it simple to get around the city and see everything.

Visit locations like the Villa Borghese Gardens, close to the Spanish Steps and the magnificent bridges that straddle the Tiber to avoid the main crowd. Ask locals in hotels or backstreet eateries to learn about some of the city's hidden gems.

THINGS TO CONSIDER

It's crucial to understand that the city has a high crime rate for pickpockets due to its attractiveness. Keep all your valuables in the hotel safe, and only bring what you need when you leave the house. Remember that you are unlikely to capture a thief after they have struck due to the sheer number of people in the area.

Rome can be expensive, so if you're thinking about going, make sure you budget enough cash. If you want to stay somewhere less expensive but still nice, consider booking a place near Stazione Termini, Rome's main train station. This will allow you to use the train to get around without the cost of the city's main area.

TOURIST SPOTS AND ATTRACTIONS,

Rome is full of tourist attractions and historic sites, offering something for everyone to see and experience. Here are some of the most popular tourist spots and attractions in Rome, with details on routes, travel times, and places to see along the way:

The Vatican: Located in Vatican City, the Vatican is home to the Sistine Chapel, the Vatican Museums, and St. Peter's Basilica. A visit here can take anywhere from half a day to a full day, depending on how much you want to see.

The Colosseum: This ancient amphitheater is one of the most recognizable landmarks in Rome and is a must-visit for history buffs. The Colosseum is located in the city's heart and can be reached by foot or public transportation.

The Roman Forum: This ancient public square was the center of ancient Rome's political, commercial, and social life. A visit here can take anywhere from an hour to half a day, depending on your interest in ancient history.

The Pantheon: This ancient temple-turned-church is one of the best-preserved ancient buildings in Rome and is a must-visit for architecture fans. The Pantheon is located in the city's heart and can be reached by foot or public transportation.

The Spanish Steps: This iconic staircase is a popular gathering place for locals and tourists alike, offering a great view of the city from the top. The Spanish Steps are located in the city's heart and can be reached by foot or public transportation.

These are just a few of Rome's many tourist spots and attractions. To get the most out of your visit, consider hiring a local guide or taking a guided tour to learn more about the history and culture of the city.

CHAPTER 6: LODGING AND TRANSPORTATION

Rome offers various lodging options, from budget-friendly hostels to luxury hotels. When it comes to transportation, there are several options for getting around the city, including:

Accommodation: There are many options for lodging in Rome, including budget-friendly hostels, mid-range hotels, and luxury hotels. It's recommended to book in advance, especially during peak tourist season, to ensure availability and get the best rates.

Public Transportation: Buses, trams, and metro lines are all part of Rome's well-functioning public transit network. Visitors can purchase a single-ride ticket or a multi-day pass for unlimited use.

Taxis: Taxis are readily available in Rome and can be hailed on the street or called in advance. It's important to note that taxis in Rome are more expensive than other forms of transportation.

Bikes: Renting a bike is a great way to see the city and explore its many parks and gardens. There are several bike rental companies located throughout Rome.

Walking: Rome is a very walkable city, and many of its main tourist attractions are close to each other. Walking is a great way to get a feel for the city and its local culture.

Choosing a mode of transportation is recommended based on your budget, the length of your stay, and your itinerary. It's also important to familiarize yourself with the local transportation system and its rules and regulations to ensure a safe and enjoyable trip.

Rome experiences rainy winters and dry, sweltering summers. 2.7 million people are living in the city. Rome is one of the Italian countries where a passport is required for entry. But if your stay isn't longer than 90 days, you don't need to be concerned about the visa. Rome is best visited between October and March, which is considered the off-season. In the summer, there are much too many visitors. Try to get a room at a hotel close to the historic centre or the centro storico. The Spanish Steps and Piazza del Popolo are conveniently close to the Hotel de Russie. By doing this, you will see these locations before moving on to other interesting locations.

Rome is situated in Central Italy's west region, not far from the ocean. The principal port of contemporary Rome is Civitavecchia, where cruise ships berth before docking in the Italian capital.

You ought to go solo exploring in Rome. Make a list of the locations you want to visit. You will find it much simpler to travel thanks to this, and you'll also be able to save time.

TramBus is available, and it's affordable and excellent. This bus system allows you to visit all the picturesque locations in and around Rome.

Rome may be reached effectively by train. The main station, Stazione Termini, is located relatively close to Rome's historic centre. There are a lot of distant stations as well, and termini are also accessible by coach. Fiumicino is Rome's primary international airport, and travellers from the US commonly travel here. It would help if you didn't drive into Rome; instead, take the train from the airport.

Since Rome has a comprehensive metro system and bus service, using public transportation to travel practically anywhere is simple. If you plan to travel in a packed metro car, be on the lookout for pickpockets. Some excellent Rome transportation maps are well worth buying if you want to use public transportation, and look for them in newsstands, tourist information centres, or gift shops. Ask for the price before getting in the cab if you decide to take one in Roma to prevent being overcharged.

Rome often enjoys a Mediterranean climate, yet it can get hot sometimes, especially in the summer. Ottobrata is the term used by Romans to describe such beautiful, bright days in Rome. Apr and May, or late Sept through early October, are the ideal times to visit Rome.

This Rome travel guide will provide all the information on the budget-friendly Rome hotels that you could want. Given the abundance of hotels in Rome, you can easily compare their costs and choose the best suits your budget. It would help if you were mindful of how much money you spend when visiting Rome, so it will be better to make your hotel reservations online rather than physically looking for accommodations once you get there.

Hotels close to the most popular tourist destinations are widely available. Still, you should make reservations as soon as possible since these hotels fill up quickly once the holiday season begins. You no longer need to worry if you have completed everything, and you can leave with your family and loved ones to enjoy a wonderful and exciting holiday.

There are countless things to do in Rome, so why not start with an open-top bus trip to gain a sense of the city and its layout before deciding how to spend the rest of your days?

TYPES OF LODGING AVAILABLE IN ROME

Rome offers a wide range of lodging options, including:

Hotels: Rome has a wide range of hotels, from budget-friendly options to luxury establishments. Hotels are typically the most popular choice for visitors and offer amenities such as room service, restaurants, and fitness centres.

Bed & Breakfasts (B&Bs): B&Bs are a great option for travellers who want a more personal and intimate experience. They typically offer a more homely atmosphere and a breakfast that is included in the price.

Rental Apartments: Rental apartments offer the flexibility and independence of having your own space. They are ideal for families or groups of travellers and offer more space and privacy than hotels or B&Bs.

Hostels: Hostels are a budget-friendly option for travellers, offering shared dorm rooms and private rooms at a lower cost. Hostels are a great option for travellers looking to meet other travellers on a tight budget.

Vacation Rentals: Vacation rentals offer a more homely and personal experience and are ideal for families or groups of travellers. They offer more space, privacy, and amenities than hotels, making them a popular option for longer stays in Rome.

It's important to consider your budget, the length of your stay, and your travel style when choosing the right type of lodging for your trip to Rome. It's recommended to research and compare different options to find the one that best suits your needs.

Hotels

AntiquaRoma Bed & Breakfast

Between the Spanish Steps and the Vatican City, the Bed & Breakfast AntiquaRoma is located in the vicinity of Castel Sant'Angelo. Please note that visitors are kindly invited to let the hotel know their intended arrival time.

The Dock inn

The Dock hotel is conveniently located near a line B underground station, and the distance between the C airports and the hotel is roughly 20 kilometres. A 10-minute walk from the underground station will get you to the hotel, and it takes a taxi five minutes.

INFORMATION ON TRANSPORTATION AVAILABLE FOR GETTING AROUND.

There are many ways to get to Rome; if you're already in Europe, a car or train will take you quickly into the centre of this magnificent city. However, be careful of traffic jams; these are best observed from the sidewalk, where you can laugh at the Romans' comical impatience and penchant for honking their cars.

The busy airport is easily accessible if you are travelling from a distance, but because it is so large, reserve a hotel room in advance.

Rome is a popular tourist destination all year long, and it is incredible how crowded the hotels are all the time. In light of this, it is a smart idea to compare prices—not just between hotels but also across booking services—and a fantastic idea to do so by using websites that compare hotel prices.

Getting around in Rome is easy with the following transportation options:

Public Transportation: Rome has an efficient public transportation system, including buses, trams, and metro lines. Visitors can purchase a single-ride ticket or a multi-day pass for unlimited use.

Taxis: Taxis are readily available in Rome and can be hailed on the street or called in advance. It's important to note that taxis in Rome are more expensive than other forms of transportation.

Bikes: Renting a bike is a great way to see the city and explore its many parks and gardens. There are several bike rental companies located throughout Rome.

Walking: Rome is a very walkable city, and many of its main tourist attractions are close to each other. Walking is a great way to get a feel for the city and its local culture.

Cars: Driving in Rome can be challenging due to narrow streets, heavy traffic, and limited parking. It is recommended to only drive in Rome if you are familiar with the city and its roads.

CONCLUSION

Rome is a stunning, old city filled with architecture and the frantic pace of Italian life. There is frequently more to see than there is time for, as the city is home to top international fashion designers' stores, some of which are tucked away near the Spanish Steps, as well as the renowned Colosseum, Trevi Fountain, and other attractions. Even though the streets of Italy's capital city are crowded, plenty of charming eateries and gorgeous Gelato shops are scattered throughout, especially if you explore some of the suburbs. This will help you truly appreciate Italian culture.

Rome is a wonderful city! Rome is undoubtedly the ideal location for any traveler because it is a city where the past and the present coexist in style.

Rome is the ideal setting, whether your goal is to visit all major sites in order or want to kick back and relax.

Be forewarned, though, as Rome becomes extremely hot in the middle of the summer. A nearby awning of a street café allows you to sit in the shade and have an icy cold local delicacy beer while doing as the Romans do and enjoying the passersby. But there is also always an icy fountain to plunge your feet into.

Here is a very short list of the attractions you must see in Rome if your stay is short—45% of all visitor journeys to the city last less than four days.

Pope Square and the Vatican. Seeing two of the most famous locations in the world at once is made possible by the Vatican's location at the north corner of the huge St. Peter's Square.

The Vatican is among the most famous destinations in the world, despite not being the largest place on earth. The Vatican is the smallest state in the world and is erected on the Tomb of St. Peter. It is also incredibly beautiful, from the Sistine Chapel's stunning display of artistic brilliance to the magnificent Gardens and Water Features.

The stunning Trevi Fountain, made famous by the sublime film Roman Holiday, is another Rome attraction not to be missed. It is located at the terminus of the Roman Aqua Virgo aqueduct, which was constructed in 19 BC, and everyone is familiar with the legend that states that if you throw a coin into the fountain, you will be guaranteed to return to Rome.

Another location worth visiting is a structure with a rather peculiar past. The Castel Sant' Angelo, which was constructed as the mausoleum for the Roman Emperor Hadrian but weirdly also served as a papal residence and a prison, albeit not simultaneously, must be said.

Try not to miss the Spanish Steps if you think the coins you threw into the Trevi Fountain won't work. The most important of all Rome's monuments, the incredible Colosseum (full ticket entrance for this year is 15.50 Euros or roughly $22.5), which was built by Emperor Vespasian 1,379 years ago—yes, 1937 years ago—it has to be written in words to be believed, actually just like Rome!

Made in the USA
Monee, IL
18 March 2023

30152597R00056